Rex Finds His ROAR!™

care center
EDUCATE & ADVOCATE

to all the brave children conquering abuse.

Copyright © 2017 The CARE Center.
All Rights Reserved. No part of this book may be reproduced in any manner without written permission except in the case of brief quotations included in critical articles and reviews. For information, please contact The CARE Center.

The CARE Center
1403 Ashton Place
Oklahoma City, OK 73117
(405) 236-2100

First published in the United States in 2017.

ISBN 9780692856000

First Edition First Printing

Illustrated by Amy Nickerson

Hey Parents!

My name is Mrs. Ashton. I am so glad you chose to read Rex Finds His ROAR! Are you ready to go on a journey with your child?

Meet Our Main Character, Rex the Lion!

Through his eyes, you will be able to talk to your child about being safe in some tough situations. Follow the steps outlined below, to use this book as a tool to talk with your kids about body safety and abuse prevention.

- First, read over the Rules of ROARing™ found in the back so you can emphasize each rule along with Rex.
- Help your child understand the lesson in Rex Finds His ROAR. Make it a fun learning experience, and let them know that like Rex, they are brave.
- Continue to ROAR! Reread the book often and have the Rules of ROARing™ conversation with your child at least four times a year.

If you have questions, need additional training or follow-up, visit us at carecenter-okc.org, or contact us at 405.236.2100 or roar@carecenter-okc.org.

© 2017 The CARE Center. All Rights Reserved.

This is Rex. He is a brave lion with a
BIG ROAR!

But something has happened to Rex. His ROAR was taken from him!

Someone he trusted and saw as a good friend touched his private area (you know, the places covered by your swimsuit and underwear) and told him to keep it a secret. Rex didn't know what to do.

His Mom told him never to keep secrets, but he was scared.

Now, Rex cannot ROAR and is very sad! Let's go on a journey with Rex. Will you help him find his ROAR?

First, Rex decided to ask his friend Roland the owl for help. He is a smart owl, so maybe he will know where to look! They searched around Roland's bedroom in his tree house.

Do you see anything?

"Look! There's an R under the blanket!"

Roland pulled back the covers to get it for Rex.

"Remember, Rex, privates are private, like parts of your body covered by a swimsuit. No one should ask to see or touch them. If someone asks you to touch or look at parts of their body that are covered by their underwear or swimsuit, say NO."

"What about my Mom or Dad?"

"Sometimes Mom, Dad or a doctor will need to touch you. This is okay, but they always need to explain why and ask first."

Rex was glad his friend Roland helped him find the first R to his ROAR. But he still had 3 more letters to look for! So he asked his good friend Olivia, a very tall giraffe, for help.

They walked to the park playground. Rex and Olivia looked by the swings, the slide, and in the jungle gym. Can you see where they found the next letter of his ROAR?

"Up there! I see the O on top of the jungle gym!"

Rex was excited to have the first two letters of his ROAR back, but he knew he needed to keep looking for the rest. He remembered to be brave and ask for help again.

He went to his friend Abbie's house. Abbie is a wise elephant, so maybe she would know where to find another letter. They searched around Abbie's swimming pool. Do you see where a letter is hiding?

Rex had 3 letters back now! He was starting to feel a lot happier. But he needed the last letter R to have all of his ROAR back. He went to his school to look for it.

Rex knew he could talk to his teacher, Mrs. Ashton. She is an adult that Rex trusts, and he feels safe in her classroom.

He searched all around Mrs. Ashton's classroom. Can you see the last missing letter?

"Rex, you've had your ROAR with you all along! You never really lost it. It has always been inside you! If something upsets you, RAISE your voice and tell someone. Use your ROAR! It helps to have 3 safe grown-ups you know, trust and can talk to anytime you feel sad, alone or scared. I am one of the people you can always talk to if you need help!"

Rex was so excited! He stood up tall and gave the

BIGGEST ROAR

you've ever heard! Rex knew he had a powerful voice. He wasn't scared of losing it anymore.

Wherever you are, wherever you go, your ROAR can keep you safe ANYWHERE!

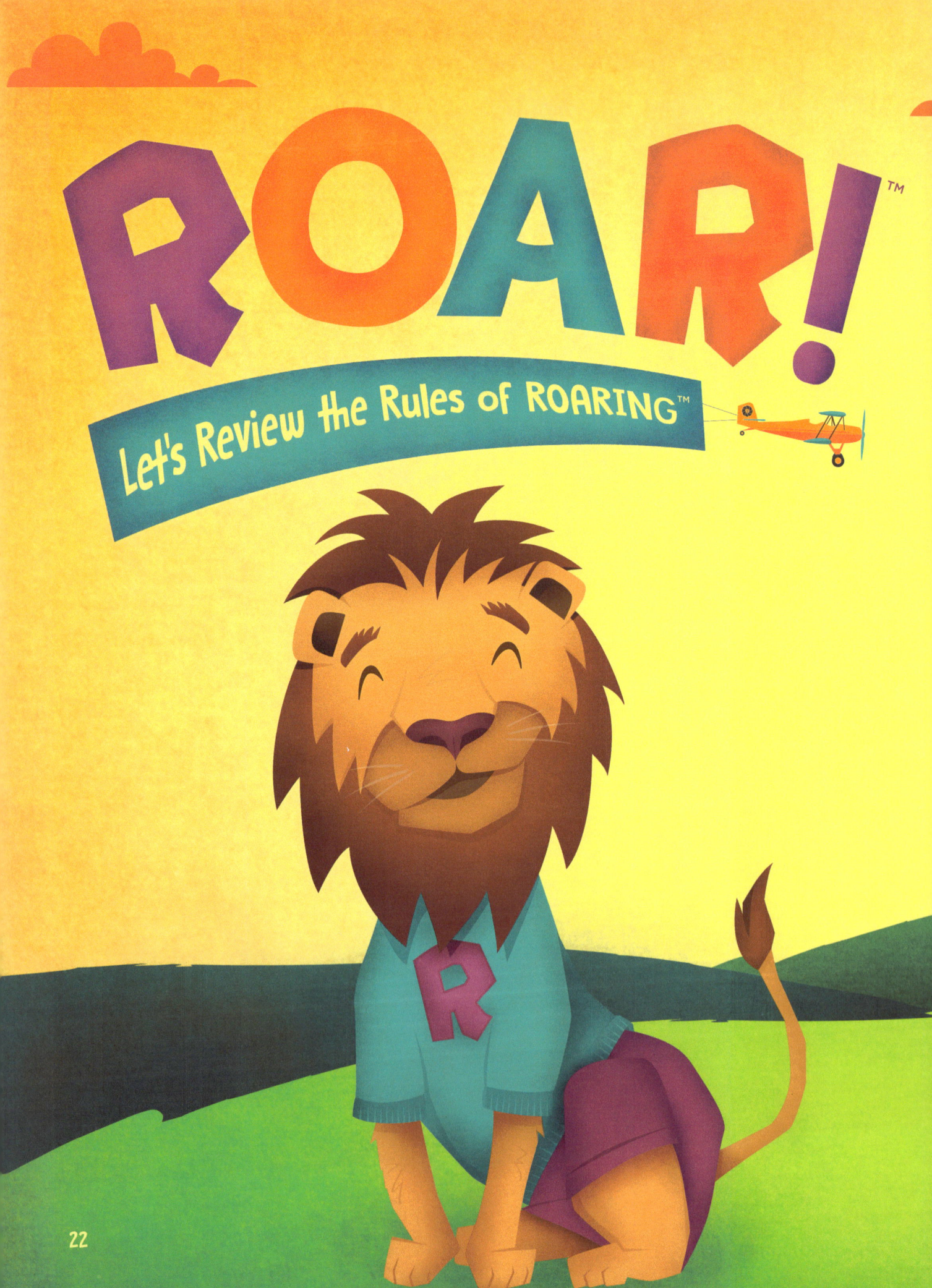

Remember, privates are private.

Okay to say no.

Always talk about secrets.

Raise your voice and tell someone.

www.ingramcontent.com/pod-product-compliance
Lightning Source LLC
Chambersburg PA
CBHW042145290426
44110CB00002B/123